Spring on the Farm

The Child's World®
childsworld.com

Published by The Child's World®
1980 Lookout Drive • Mankato, MN 56003-1705
800-599-READ • www.childsworld.com

Photographs ©: iStockphoto, cover, 1; Shutterstock Images, 5, 6–7, 8, 11, 12, 14–15, 16–17; SoSzPhoto/ Shutterstock Images, 18; Nate Allred/Shutterstock Images, 21

Design Element: Shutterstock Images

ISBN 9781503816572
LCCN 2016945629

Printed in the United States of America
PA02324

ABOUT THE AUTHOR
M. J. York is a writer and editor from Minnesota. She enjoys spring rains and planting her garden.

Contents

Spring Morning

It is spring. A farmer wakes up. She feeds the horses.

Planting

Spring is warm. It is time to plant **crops**.

The farmer drives a **tractor**. It pulls a machine for planting. It plants seeds.

Some farmers plant vegetables. Others plant wheat.

11

It rains often in spring.

Soon the plants grow.

Baby Animals

Farm animals are born in spring. The farmer helps care for them.

Piglets are born. There are many in a **litter**.

Chicks hatch from eggs.

They peck in the yard.

Calves learn to walk. They play in the spring grass.

Fluffy Lamb Craft

Make a fluffy lamb with your handprint!

Supplies:

black construction paper	scissors
	cotton balls
white crayon	glue

Instructions:

1. Trace your handprint onto the black paper. Use your white crayon.

2. Cut out your handprint. Flip it upside down.

3. Glue cotton balls all over. Leave the tips of the fingers bare.

4. Draw eyes and a mouth on the thumb piece.

Glossary

crops — (KRAHPS) Crops are plants grown for food. Farmers plant crops in spring.

litter — (LIT-ur) A litter is a group of baby animals born at the same time. A litter can have many piglets.

tractor — (TRAK-tur) A tractor is a machine. A tractor pulls other farm machines.

To Learn More

Books

Brown, Laaren. *Animal Planet Farm Animals*. New York, NY: Time, 2016.

Cooper, Elisha. *Farm*. New York, NY: Orchard Books, 2010.

Dickmann, Nancy. *Food from Farms*. Chicago, IL: Heinemann Library, 2011.

Web Sites

Visit our Web site for links about spring on the farm: **childsworld.com/links**

Note to Parents, Teachers, and Librarians: We routinely verify our Web links to make sure they are safe and active sites. So encourage your readers to check them out!

Index